D0793496

# Certitude

# Certitude

*A Profusely Illustrated*
## GUIDE
### TO
*Blockheads and Bullheads,*
## PAST & PRESENT

———————————— ◾ ————————————

### Adam Begley

ILLUSTRATIONS BY
### Edward Sorel

INTRODUCTION BY
### *Christopher Hitchens*

◾

*Design by Walter Bernard*

HARMONY BOOKS ◆◆ NEW YORK

www.crownpublishing.com

Harmony Books is a registered trademark
and the Harmony Books colophon
is a trademark of Random House, Inc.

The illustration "The Bush Gang" was originally published in *Vanity Fair,*
and the illustrations "Aimee Semple McPherson" and "John Brown"
were originally published in *The New Yorker.*

Library of Congress Cataloging-in-Publication Data
Begley, Adam.
Certitude A profusely illlustrated guide to blockheads and bullheads,
past & present / Adam Begley ; illustrations by Edward Sorel.—1st ed.
1. Biography—Anecdotes. 2. World history—Anecdotes.
3. Certainty—Anecdotes. I. Sorel, Edward, 1929– II. Title.
CT105.B39 2009
909—dc22          2008051786

ISBN 978-0-307-40804-4

Printed in the United States of America

Design by Walter Bernard

1 3 5 7 9 10 8 6 4 2

First Edition

# Contents

# Introduction: Certitude and Its Discontents

*by* Christopher Hitchens

You sometimes hear people saying to their antagonists in debates on this or that topic: "I envy you your certainty." One presumes that the origins of this expression must be ironic or even merely sarcastic, but there are also, rather touchingly, those who employ it literally and as a compliment. There are also those who, faced with doubt in its lack-of-faith form, will try to turn the tables by saying that unbelief is itself a form of fundamentalism. (This has lately become a favorite cheap debating trick of the religious Right.) By definition, of course, non-belief cannot be classified as a faith—and it's interesting to speculate about the degree of subconscious self-hatred that may exist in a religious person who taunts an atheist with being no better than a "believer"! —whereas the person of faith must aver not only that there is a god, but that this god's wishes and desires may be known. It can be stated confidently, for example, that he hates hams and clams and was otherwise engaged when homosexuals (who are somehow "against nature") were created. In other words, the less evidence we possess, the more absolutely sure we must be.

Certitude of this kind is by no means to be envied, and those who have for years been relishing Edward Sorel's occasional cartoon-update "Religion in the News" will know what a rich seam of absurdity and worse can be mined from the credulous. (*Credulous* means, really, "one who craves certitude.") Many of this fine book's prime exhibits are necessarily also of the "faith-based" sort, and when confronted with the claims of such jackasses and poltroons it is always wise to keep in mind the work of David Hume on miracles. When confronted with an apparent miracle, remarked the great Scottish philosopher, it is prudent to ask oneself which is more likely: that the rules of nature have been suspended or that you yourself are under a misapprehension. Doubt, in such an instance, is the mind's best friend. Certitude, by contrast, betrays the wish to be mindless. The case of Sir Arthur Conan Doyle's unshakeable belief in fairies is not precisely an instance of religious tomfoolery but does show that certain kinds of belief are evidence-proof. The actual case was even more bizarre than Adam Begley has room to say; even the good folks at Kodak declared themselves taken in by the pathetically obvious darkroom hoax. The most sorry illusions and delusions have a way of spreading in a way that, alas for suffering humanity, cannot be copied by moments of lucidity.

Let's not be snobbish about the deluded. There may be crowds of what H.L. Mencken called "boobs," who will stand in line to buy colored medicine water and let their jaws hang low at apparitions of the Virgin. But the great William Butler Yeats was never happier than at spiritualist séances that featured burblings (and scribblings) from the beyond. The hardheaded Henry Ford was an abject pushover for that preposterous hoax *The Protocols of the Learned Elders of Zion,* and not only fell for it himself but invested a huge tranche of valuable capital in trying to get others to become true believers, too. By the way, congratulations to Begley for getting this right and describing the *Protocols* as a "hoax": They are too-often referred to as a "forgery" whereas a forgery is a copy of something authentic, and not a mere fabrication.

When you have finished scanning David Hume on miracles you might like to take up Richard Hofstadter's work on *The Paranoid Style in American Politics.* Here you will find the best definition of the paranoid that I have yet read: a man "who already has all the information he needs." Again in these pages you will be put in mind of the phenomenon, and again you will find that much of the pathology is "faith-based." Did Elijah Muhammad have to prove that every blue-eyed white devil actually possessed blue eyes? Not really. Best to regard it as a metaphor. But would he revisit the general, overarching theory that all whites of all eye colors were essentially diabolical? Never!

Something of the same effect can be observed with the "infallibility" concept. This higher by-product of certitude means that it can be very difficult to correct a mistake. In my own lifetime I have seen a series of popes make public apologies to Jews (for the false charge of "deicide" and its consequences), to Protestants (for the Counter-Reformation), to Galileo, to forcibly converted and exterminated South American Indians, to Eastern Orthodox Christians (for the massacres in the Balkans), and to Muslims (for the Crusades). But having made these little course-corrections, inevitable perhaps in the life of a "one true Church," the Vatican is now ready to go back to being infallible all over again. So that one day if—just suppose—it is discovered that AIDS was a worse affliction than the condom, rather than the other way around, the necessary admission will have to be delayed for years by the fact that there was once a sacred dogma involved.

Nobody likes a ditherer. Both military and political leadership are best exercised by people who can make a decision and stick to it, rather than (as was once said of Lord Derby) "like a cushion, bear the impression of whoever last sat upon him." However, a decided leader who does not listen to the doubts of others as well as his own may well become famous for other reasons. From George Armstrong Custer to the teak-headed British generals on the Western Front, we have shining examples of those who kept doing the same old thing, each time hoping for a different result. This conforms to George Santayana's definition of fanaticism, which is "redoubling your efforts when you have forgotten your aims." Only the wonderful consolation of knowing that you were right all along can get you through an ordeal like that. If it were not so, there would be no memoir industry and no "second act" racket in which gruesome exhibits like "the new Nixon" can be dragged onto the amphitheater's already bloodstained sand.

I have some Humean disagreements with the authors here. (Which is more likely, that a Saddam Hussein who had both used and concealed WMDs would be telling the truth just for once, or once again concealing his hand?) But that's because I think the same standard should apply to everyone, including myself. One day, perhaps, the Virgin Mary will appear in blue raiment with good visibility and on camera to a large throng of adult non-Catholics, and will speak intelligible words. On that day, if I am present, I will be inclined to think that I am suffering from an individual or collective hallucination. In fact, on balance, I'll be absolutely sure of it.

"To be positive: to be mistaken
at the top of one's voice."
—AMBROSE BIERCE

"Convictions are more dangerous
enemies of truth than lies."
—FRIEDRICH NIETZSCHE

"Doubt is not a pleasant condition,
but certainty is an absurd one."
—VOLTAIRE

# Certitude

# Pope Urban II
## (1042–99)

On November 27, 1095, the tenth day of the Council of Clermont, Pope Urban II (a.k.a. Otho, Otto, or Odo of Lagery) gave a sermon historians now consider one of the most important in the history of Europe. By declaring a "bellum sacrum" (what Muslims call "jihad") against the "infidels" occupying the Holy Land, he launched the First Crusade, a bloody rampage through Europe and Asia Minor, which, unlike subsequent crusades, actually achieved its purpose: to regain control of Jerusalem. The crusaders celebrated the capture of the Sacred City with a comprehensive, notoriously ferocious massacre of all its inhabitants—Muslims, Jews, and even a few stray Christians.

You could be forgiven for failing to suppress a cry of historical anguish: *What was Odo thinking?* The answer depends on which version of his speech you prefer. There are a half dozen of them, all transcribed years after the event—after the pontiff's death and after Jerusalem had been "liberated" (which of course conferred a retrospective righteousness on the entire sordid adventure).

One account suggests that the pope was essentially exporting violence: "Let those who have been fighting against their brothers and relatives now fight in a proper way against the barbarians." In another, he rages against the crimes purportedly committed by Muslims in the Holy Land: "They circumcise the Christians, and the blood of the circumcision they either spread upon the altars or pour into the vases of the baptismal font. When they wish to torture people by a base death, they perforate their navels, and dragging forth the extremity of the intestines, bind it to a stake; then with flogging they lead the victim around until the viscera having gushed forth the victim falls prostrate upon the ground." There's no mention, however, of WMD.

In yet another account, Urban seems to be calling for suicide attacks: It is a "beautiful thing," he says, "to die for Christ in that city in which He died for us."

But Odo's fixation with Jerusalem was also geographic: He believed it to be the center of the earth (in one account, he repeats the claim for emphasis).

Everyone agrees that he promised immediate remission of sins for those who died in battle against the "pagans" (though he said nothing about flocks of virgins awaiting them in paradise). And there's general agreement that the sermon was a wild success with the three hundred-odd clerics at the council, who took up a cry that perhaps best distills Urban's message: *Deus vult*— God wills it.

Compare that sublime certainty with the Arabic phrase we've all grown familiar with in recent years: *Inshallah*—*If* God wills it.

# Carry A. Nation
## (1846–1911)

Armed with her trademark hatchet (before that she used brickbats, rocks, and the odd billiard ball), Carry Nation would storm into a saloon and demolish it, an unstoppable force fueled by unyielding rage against intoxicating drink. Even more astonishing than the naked fury with which this fifty-four-year-old grandmother pursued her agenda—from 1900 to 1910 she wrecked dozens and dozens of bars, first in Kansas and then across the country—is the effectiveness of her tornado-style protest. Call her the anti-Gandhi—through violence, she galvanized the temperance movement and set in motion the political process that in 1919 gave us the 18th Amendment: Prohibition.

She was not given to self-doubt: "I am appointed

for this," she wrote in her autobiography, *The Use and Need of the Life of Carry A. Nation,* and if anyone wondered exactly who appointed her, she set them straight by calling herself the "bulldog of Jesus." She was arrested more than thirty times, beaten, pelted with rotten eggs, and ridiculed. Never for a minute did she question the wisdom of her mission or wonder about the consequences of success.

She died eight years before the constitutional ban on liquor dried up every state in the union (with disastrous results, perverse effects on a grand scale)—but it's safe to say that had she lived, Carry Nation would have been dissatisfied with the fruit of her labor. Prohibition, she might have said, was a half measure, feebly enforced. She'd have scoffed at anything less than a total ban—policed, one supposes, by hatchet-wielding harpies.

# Martin Luther
## (1483–1546)

Maybe Martin Luther never did nail his world-shaking Ninety-five Theses to the door of the castle church in Wittenberg; or maybe he did, but doing so was simply standard practice—the 1517 equivalent of blogging. And yet there's something in the image of the stern young theologian tapping forcefully with his hammer that captures the determined spirit of his reformist zeal.

Now picture him battering away in a furious, spitting rage, howling curses and barking gutter insults. That's Martin Luther when he turns his attention to the Jews.

Unless you read for yourself his long, vile rant *On the Jews and Their Lies*, which he wrote just three years before his death, it's hard to believe that so much undisguised hatred could pour out of a man who gave his name to a branch of the Christian church.

His advice on how to rid the land of the "unbearable, devilish burden of the Jews"? Burn their synagogues and schools to the ground; raze and destroy their houses; confiscate their prayer books and Talmudic writings; forbid their rabbis to teach "on pain of loss of life and limb"; deny them safe conduct on the highways; ban usury; force them to do manual labor. And the kicker: "If this does not help we must drive them out like mad dogs."

Luther didn't think up yellow stars or cattle cars or gas chambers—but those who did turned to him to justify their deeds.

# Arthur Conan Doyle
## (1859–1930)

Everyone recognizes Sherlock Holmes by the pipe and the hat, but the detective's distinguishing trait is his unfailing logic, the brilliance of his deductive reasoning. And what of Arthur Conan Doyle, the struggling young doctor who created Holmes in 1887? Was Conan Doyle as lucidly rational and piercingly perceptive as the character he invented? Not quite.

A lapsed Catholic in his youth, in later life Conan Doyle became a dedicated Spiritualist. He called it a "sacred cause" and wrote a whole shelf of books making the case that it's entirely possible for the living to communicate with the spirits of the dead. One of his books on the supernatural, *The Coming of the Fairies*, is an ardent brief on behalf of a handful of photographs taken by two teenage girls; the photos purported to show fairies—cute little winged creatures—frolicking in a garden in the Yorkshire village of Cottingley.

It's difficult, at this distance in time, to believe that anyone, let alone the creator of Sherlock Holmes, could entertain even for a moment the idea that the Cottingley fairies might actually exist, and that the photographs—featuring sweetly innocent girls and what look exactly like paper-cutout fairies—were anything other than a hoax. (At the very end of their lives, decades after Conan Doyle's death, the girls recanted: The fairies were indeed just pieces of cleverly painted paper.)

If only Sherlock Holmes could have communicated with his credulous creator and repeated the line he used so often with Dr. Watson: "You know my methods. Apply them."

# Prosper-René Blondlot
## (1849–1930)

A distinguished French scientist and head of the physics department at the university in his hometown of Nancy, René Blondlot was conducting experiments on the newly discovered X-ray in the spring of 1903 when out of the corner of his eye he noticed a detector spark glowing more brightly than it should have. He realized at once that this was his Eureka moment, that he'd discovered a new kind of radiation. He called it the N-ray, in honor of his place of birth.

The news was greeted with great excitement in physics labs all over Europe. Ingenious experiments were devised to demonstrate that N-rays emanate from all sorts of substances, including the human body (especially from tensed muscles and nerves). Unfortunately, the trick of catching the variations in luminosity that signaled the presence of N-rays was not straightforward—literally: One had to look sideways, and have good eyes.

The Académie des Sciences had seen enough: It had already announced that Blondlot was to receive its top prize when a young American physicist visited the labs in Nancy and proved conclusively that the experiments were a sham. What Blondlot was seeing was a function of peripheral vision, in other words, purely subjective.

Asked to participate in a new round of experiments, Blondlot declined, saying, "The phenomena are too delicate." Nothing would ever shake his faith in what he'd seen with his own eyes. But the N-ray, alas, was no more.

# Ayn Rand
## (1905–82)

When Mike Wallace interviewed her on national television in 1959, Ayn Rand was fifty-four, a bestselling novelist, founder of her very own philosophical movement, Objectivism, and the adored heroine of a growing band of acolytes (among them Alan Greenspan). She was also a very scary person. It wasn't just the thick Russian accent (which she never lost), or the rictus she presented in lieu of a smile, or even the crazed ricochet movement of her large dark eyes—what was scariest was her poorly concealed preoccupation with an unseen audience: She couldn't help glancing away from Wallace and straight into the lens of the camera.

"You have no faith in anything," Wallace objected, "only in your mind."

"That is not faith," Rand replied. "That is a conviction."

At the time of the interview, Rand was engaged

in an extramarital affair with a much younger man—twenty-five years younger, to be precise. The affair dragged on until 1968, when the erstwhile boy-toy (who had become a tireless promoter of Objectivism) hooked up with a young actress. When Rand found out about it, the apostle of rational self-interest lost any vestige of rational cool: She flipped—publicly, angrily—disowning her protégé but not owning up to the cause of her sudden fury.

Having espoused selfishness as a moral virtue, she found the selfishness of another intolerable. A paradox presented itself: Ego, it seems, can get in the way of self-interest.

# John Cleves Symmes
## (1779–1829)

Not everyone finds concentric circles compelling, but for John Symmes they were the key to a great discovery: "The earth," he declared in 1818, "is hollow and habitable within." This simple formula (and the less simple pseudoscientific theory he elaborated) became the obsessive focus of the last twenty years of his life. On his death, his dutiful son marked his grave in Hamilton, Ohio, with a Hollow Earth monument—an obelisk with a sphere resting on top (the sphere, which has a hole drilled through it, looks a bit like a pitted olive).

A hero in the War of 1812, Symmes was an otherwise unremarkable man, with little formal education, an unprepossessing appearance, and a bad case of stage fright. And yet his lectures and "circulars" (not surprisingly, he preferred the term "circular" to "pamphlet") were convincing enough to earn him a minor celebrity. Despite poor health and his dread of crowds, he lectured in frontier towns and across New England; the aim of all his relentless proselytizing was to launch an expedition to the Arctic, where he believed one could gain access to the worlds within our world.

Though ridiculed by scientists and the press, Symmes garnered enough popular support for his polar venture to bring a petition before the Senate in 1822—but a motion to refer the matter to the Committee on Foreign Relations was tabled. Imagine if Symmes's ideas had been referred to the Department of the Interior.... (Alas, it was only established by Congress in 1849.)

# Norman Mailer
## (1923–2007)

For the first thirty-odd years of his life, Norman Mailer wrote, his "pride...was to be an atheist." But in his mid-fifties (around the time he began corresponding with Jack Abbott, the convicted killer whose parole he successfully, tragically engineered), he began rethinking his relationship with the Almighty. In *Pieces and Pontifications*, a collection of essays published in 1982 (the year Jack Abbott was tried for the murder he committed just one month into his parole), Mailer explored a new faith: He conceived of a god who is not all-powerful—but who shares power, in fact, with the Devil.

As he explained decades later, literary celebrity gave him an inkling of what it might be like to be a fallible God: "Obviously," he conceded, "a celebrity is a long, long, long, long way from the celestial, but nonetheless it does...[give] you power that you usually don't know how to use well. So the parallel was stronger than I realized."

Over the years, his beliefs hardened into doctrine. Less than a month before his death in 2007, he published *On God: An Uncommon Conversation*—his last testament, as it were—in which he lays out in impressive detail his private theology, the cornerstone of which is a fallible deity with a particular professional orientation: "God is an artist. And like an artist, God has successes, God has failures."

As Montesquieu remarked, "If the triangles had a god, they would give it three sides."

# Empress Alexandra Fyodorovna
## (1872–1918)

In 1904, after giving birth to four daughters in succession, Czarina Alexandra Fyodorovna at last brought forth a male heir, Alexei Nikolaevich Romanov—but the baby, it soon became apparent, suffered from hemophilia.

When doctors proved powerless to treat the disease, Alexandra turned to faith healers—in particular Grigori Rasputin, a Siberian peasant-turned-monk thought by some to have mystic powers and by others to be a shockingly oversexed charlatan. The czar and czarina soon convinced themselves that when Rasputin prayed for their ailing son, his condition improved.

In 1912, while the royal family were at their hunting estate in eastern Poland, Alexei suffered a life-threatening hemorrhage. A desperate Alexandra telegraphed Rasputin, begging for his intercession. He promised that the future czar would get well: "Don't let the doctors bother him too much; let him rest," he cabled back—and lo, the boy recovered. The czarina was hooked.

Though false, the widespread rumor that she and Rasputin were lovers was profoundly damaging. By the time Nicholas II set off for the front during World War I—leaving his wife in charge of the government—the monk, vodka soaked, notorious for accepting bribes, was arguably the most powerful man in St. Petersburg.

In December 1916, a conspiracy of nobles, dismayed by his undiminished sway over Alexandra, arranged to have Rasputin killed. Three months later, the czar was deposed by the Bolsheviks; a year after that, Nicholas, Alexandra, and their children were executed.

# Madonna
## (b. 1958)

**M**adonna doesn't believe in death. With a name like that, why would she?

News that the queen of pop was not just a material girl began to spread in 1997, after she gave a cocktail party at the headquarters of her record company to promote the Kabbalah Center, an organization (some would say cult) dedicated to the dissemination of the ancient teachings (some would say mumbo jumbo) of the mystic branch of Judaism. Madonna embraced Kabbalah, she told the guests at her party, when she had been pregnant, exhausted from making the movie *Evita,* and in need of some kind of anchor. Since then she has become a great benefactor of the Kabbalah Center, donating many millions—and allowing it to bask in the reflected glory of her multiplatinum aura.

In return she gets life everlasting. According to the Zohar, the key text of Kabbalah, our souls "reenter the

absolute substance whence they have emerged. But to accomplish this end they must develop all the perfections... and if they have not fulfilled this condition during one life, they must commence another, a third, and so forth, 'til they have acquired the condition which fits them for reunion with God." In plain English, we're recycled 'til we get it right. Or plainer still, *she'll be back*. And she's been here before: The good people at the Kabbalah Center have reportedly convinced Madonna that she's the reincarnation of the biblical queen Esther.

# Donald Rumsfeld
## (b. 1932)

In an administration notoriously impervious to doubt, Secretary of Defense Donald Rumsfeld stood out as more certain than the rest. Even ignorance was for him an opportunity to show off a decisive control of the situation: "As we know, there are known knowns; there are things we know we know. We also know there are known unknowns; that is to say we know there are some things we do not know. But there are also unknown unknowns—the ones we don't know we don't know." Contained and neutralized by this tidy taxonomy, the unknown unknowns were ignored—

especially when it came to the certainty to which he gave his name: the Rumsfeld Doctrine.

Thomas Friedman coined the term (and defined it: "Just enough troops to lose"), but we all recognize it as an arrogant refusal to prepare for contingency. The Iraq war was a testing ground for his adamant belief that a smaller force (less than 150,000) could defeat the Iraqi army, control a population of more than 24 million, and secure a nation the size of California. He strenuously resisted the arguments of generals who called for the deployment of several hundred thousand troops.

A month before the invasion, asked to estimate the duration of the war, Rumsfeld answered, "It is unknowable how long that conflict will last. It could last six days, six weeks. I doubt six months." Stuff happens.

# Pope Leo X
## (1475–1521)

Ⅰn the mid-sixteenth century, John Bale, Bishop of Ossory, cited an exchange between Pietro Bembo and Giovanni di Lorenzo de' Medici (a.k.a. Pope Leo X). Bembo quoted scripture at Leo, to which the pope replied: "How very profitable this fable of Christ has been to us through the ages."

We can't be certain—we're barred by our devotion to doubt—but we're confident that even if he never actually uttered the infamous words ascribed to him 430-odd years ago, the sentiment is pure Leo. It could have been his credo.

As pope, he lived high on the hog; during his seven-year reign, he spent ducats at a rate unmatched in the history of the Holy See. We're talking excess that would make Caligula blush: banquets, hunting parties, festivals, and a pervasive mood of rampant licentiousness. (As for his personal sexual proclivities, one contemporary historian observed that the pontiff "was exceedingly devoted...to that kind of pleasure that for honor's sake may not be named.")

How to fund such reckless extravagance? One solution was to sell indulgences, a way of profiting from the "fable of Christ" that incensed a young Augustinian monk named Martin Luther. Hence the Reformation....

Perhaps a last sonorous word of censure should go to the great church historian Philip Schaff: "Leo despoiled his high office of its sacredness and prostituted it into a vehicle of his own carnal propensities."

# Charlton Heston
## (1923–2008)

You wouldn't believe it, looking back over his fifteen years of unblinking support for the National Rifle Association (of which he eventually became president), but once upon a time, Charlton Heston was capable of changing his mind. Early on, for example, he was opposed to the whole concept of activist movie stars. Then, in the early 1960s, he marched in support of civil rights and endorsed Democratic candidates. In 1968, in the wake of Robert Kennedy's assassination, he joined Gregory Peck and James Stewart in calling for *stronger* gun control legislation.

Twenty years later, he had become the gun lobby's preferred celebrity spokesman, host of the annual Charlton Heston Celebrity Shoot (a three-day extravaganza featuring many pulverized clay pigeons, a handgun competition, and a smattering of Hollywood stars). From the late 1980s on, Heston was the nation's most prominent defender of the Second Amendment.

How convinced was he of the people's right to bear arms? He liked to fire up the NRA faithful with this signature flourish: Standing at the podium, he'd raise a rifle over his head and thunder, in his famous baritone, "From my cold, dead hands!" (That's short, in case you're wondering, for "I'll give you my gun when you take it from my cold, dead hands!")

In December 1998, when Heston was made president of the NRA, Mike Wallace interviewed him on *60 Minutes* and asked about his previous support for gun control. Heston replied, "I've made a number of mistakes in my life, Mike."

# Emma Goldman
## (1869–1940)

Our favorite radical, "Red Emma" wavered in some of her political convictions (she changed her mind, for instance, about the Bolsheviks). She also found that her feelings of jealousy and possessiveness vis-à-vis her lover ran counter to her professed belief in free love ("I stand condemned before the bar of my own reason," she wrote with commendable candor).

And she vacillated on the question of violence (though she was happy to help her boyfriend attempt an assassination of Henry Clay Frick, in later life she preferred less drastic measures). But there were two constants in her life: anarchism and action. Every word, every gesture was meant to further the anarchist agenda, and she never stopped speaking, never stopped *doing*. "The true revolutionist," she wrote, "will not shrink from anything to serve the Cause."

In her autobiography, *Living My Life,* Goldman tells the story of her decision, at age twenty-three, to help fund the plot to kill Frick by selling her body: The first man she managed to pick up took her to a bar and told her bluntly that she didn't have "the knack" for prostitution. " 'You haven't got it, that's all there is to it,' he assured me. He took out a ten-dollar bill and put it down before me. 'Take this and go home,' he said. . . . I was too astounded for speech." And that was the end of her career as a hooker.

# Charles Augustus Lindbergh
## (1902–74)

Heroic aviator Charles Lindbergh went to Germany in 1936 to assess the strength of the Luftwaffe. Hermann Göring helped him out. Lindbergh was impressed by everything he saw; in fact, in 1938 he decided to move his family to Germany. He found a house in Wannsee, outside Berlin. Then came *Kristallnacht;* concerned by the anti-Jewish riots, he canceled his plans. (But he kept his medal awarded "by order of der Führer," the Service Cross of the German Eagle.)

In April 1939, on his journey home from Europe, Lindbergh wrote in his diary, "a few Jews add strength and character to our country, but too many create chaos. And we are getting too many." Four months later, he noted that "whenever the Jewish percentage of total population becomes too high, a reaction seems to invariably occur."

He was feeling his way toward a powerful certitude, which found public expression at last in a speech delivered on October 13, 1939: "Our bond with Europe is a bond of race and not of political ideology....Racial strength is vital, politics a luxury." At the same time he was writing an article for *Reader's Digest* in which he stressed the need to preserve the "White race...in a pressing sea of Yellow, Black, and Brown" and guard against "the infiltration of inferior blood."

But he never doubted that "a few Jews of the right type are...an asset to any country."

# George Armstrong Custer
## (1839–76)

The doubt and conjecture that surround historical accounts of the battle of Little Bighorn dishonor the man whose unshakable self-esteem caused the catastrophe: George Armstrong Custer would have despised the tedious tangle of claim and counterclaim.

Here are the facts that matter: Having turned down the offer of Gatling guns and two additional companies of cavalry, having been repeatedly warned by his scouts that the Indian village on the banks of the Little Bighorn

River was large—larger than any they'd seen in thirty years—General Custer, confident that the Seventh Cavalry could defeat any number of Sioux and Cheyenne warriors, hurried to attack anyway, the reckless charge being the one and only military tactic in his repertoire.

He split his forces into three columns and left one company behind to guard the pack train. Not a single one of the two-hundred-odd men under his personal command survived.

Nobody denies that he was brave. Effortlessly flamboyant, with a mean, unpredictable temper and an unquenchable thirst for glory, he was a major general (by brevet appointment) by the time he was twenty-three.

His last stand was also his first defeat: Custer's famous luck had run out.

As he looked down from the bluffs at the vast Indian encampment, he said, "Hurrah, boys, we've got them." In a sense, those were his final words—the last any survivor heard him utter. And perhaps that appalling expression of hubris should be his epitaph, too.

# Jeannette Rankin
## (1880–1973)

Daughter of a Montana rancher, eldest of eleven children, Jeannette Rankin was a suffragette and a progressive who ran for Congress in 1916 (before women had won the constitutional right to vote)—she was elected, and thereby became the first female to serve in the House of Representatives.

Just four days after taking office, she joined forty-nine others in voting against U.S. entry into World War I. "I want to stand by my country," she said, "but I cannot vote for war."

Her unwavering pacifism, once American troops landed in Europe, was predictably unpopular. The *Helena Independent* denounced her as "a dagger in the hands of the German propagandists, a dupe of the Kaiser, a member of the Hun army in the United States, and a crying schoolgirl." (It was alleged that she cried during the key roll call, though eyewitnesses denied it.)

She lost a Senate bid in 1918 and retired from politics, only to return in 1940, when armies were clashing anew in Europe. Elected to the House, she was once again called upon to cast her vote for war—this time, it was the day after Pearl Harbor. Once again she said no—this time the lone dissenting voice. The hostility of the crowds, as she left the Capitol, was such that she had to seek refuge in a phone booth; the police escorted her back to her office.

Her political career was in tatters, her principles intact.

# Joseph Stalin
## (1878–1953)

Soviet spies around the world saw it coming: They flooded the Kremlin with news of an impending German invasion. For instance, in mid-April an agent stationed in Prague predicted that the offensive would begin in the second half of June. Stalin refused to believe it. He dismissed the Prague report with an angry scrawl: "English provocation! Investigate!"

Right on cue (June 22, 1941), the Wehrmacht launched Operation Barbarossa, a massive assault that inflicted staggering losses on the unprepared Red Army. It's one of the great military disasters in history.

How could Stalin—cunning, paranoid Stalin—have been blind to Hitler's intention? He was convinced that Germany, having lost the last war, would never again fight on two fronts. So long as it was at war with the West, he insisted, Germany would honor its nonaggression pact with the Soviet Union.

Fooling Stalin proved surprisingly easy: When Hitler moved more than three million soldiers to the Soviet border, the German government innocently explained that the troops were now safe from RAF bombs and that the stockpiling of troops and supplies was meant to dupe the British into thinking that an invasion of Russia was imminent. In fact, the Germans confided, it was Britain they planned to invade.

Utterly hoodwinked, Stalin hesitated in the hours after Operation Barbarossa had begun: He wanted to make sure the attack had been sanctioned by Hitler, that it wasn't the work of a rogue general.

# Nancy Davis Reagan
## (b. 1921)

The cover of *Time* magazine on May 16, 1988, featured a Polaroid snapshot of Nancy Reagan wafting through the night sky above Washington. The First Lady was looking up at the stars with the same rapt adoration—they called it "the Gaze"—with which she used to watch her husband at the podium. The headline read: "Astrology in the White House."

The magazine cover coincided with the publication of the memoirs of Ronald Reagan's former chief of staff, with whom Nancy had feuded. The disgruntled minion revealed to the world the extent of Nancy's influence over her husband's administration—and the celestial nature of that influence.

It seems that after the 1981 assassination attempt on poor Ronnie, Nancy was deeply worried about him. So she consulted her astrologer. Thereafter, the president's comings and goings were arranged—unbeknownst to him—in accordance with an astrological chart showing the "good" and "bad" days. No public event could be scheduled without the prior approval of Nancy's "friend," as the astrologer (Joan Quigley) was known.

In 1987, for instance, when Reagan met with Mikhail Gorbachev in Washington, D.C., the charts of both leaders were consulted and it was determined that 2:00 P.M. on December 8 was the ideal moment. The entire summit was built around that hour.

World peace has yet to be achieved. The fault, dear Nancy, is not in our stars, but in ourselves....

# Edgar Degas
## (1834–1917)

To say that some of his best friends were Jewish is, in the case of the great Impressionist Edgar Degas, simply the truth. From age eleven, when they met at their Paris lycée, he and Ludovic Halévy were inseparable; thirty years later, Degas was still having dinner at the Halévys once a week, and lunch just as often.

The Halévys were Jewish; Degas was not, and in 1894, when the Dreyfus Affair erupted, a fifty-year friendship came to an abrupt end.

All of France divided into two camps: the Dreyfusards, who believed in the innocence of Alfred Dreyfus, the Jewish artillery officer convicted of treason on trumped-up charges and sentenced to life imprisonment on Devil's Island; and the anti-Dreyfusards, who were wrongly convinced of his guilt.

Degas was an extreme anti-Dreyfusard: Not only was he adamant in his belief that the French military courts could never have been mistaken in convicting Captain Dreyfus, but he also felt that the Jewish population of France should suffer punishment for the crimes Dreyfus committed. He broke off contact with his fellow painters Camille Pissarro and Mary Cassatt with whom he'd been close friends—Pissarro because his father's family was Jewish, Cassatt because she was outspoken in her defense of Dreyfus.

In 1906, a court of appeals officially exonerated Dreyfus: He was readmitted into the army, promoted, and made a Chevalier of the Légion d'Honneur. Still, Edgar Degas refused to acknowledge his innocence.

# Anthony Comstock
## (1844–1915)

I t's a tough job, legislating morality. But you get results—just ask Anthony Comstock. Proud of his work as the founder of the New York Society for the Suppression of Vice, prouder still to have given his name to the Comstock Act of 1873 (which made it a federal crime to send through the mail "obscene, lewd, or lascivious" materials—not just pornography but also educational information about birth control and abortion), Comstock looked back on four decades of his antiporn crusade and listed his accomplishments: "I have convicted persons enough to fill a passenger train of sixty-one coaches, sixty coaches containing sixty passengers each and the sixty-first almost full. I have destroyed 160 tons of obscene literature."

As a special agent of the U.S. Post Office, Comstock had police powers; and he was armed, thanks to the New York State legislature, with a gun. He wielded the power

of life and death. He boasted of having driven certain purveyors of the lewd and lascivious to suicide, among them Ida Craddock, the author of sex manuals such as *The Wedding Night* and *Right Marital Living*. Craddock killed herself rather than serve a five-year sentence for the circulation of those "obscene" materials.

But a nagging question remains: After all the convictions and bannings and suicides, has vice actually been suppressed? Picture Comstock today, dressed as always all in black and sporting his famous muttonchop whiskers, clicking through the unending supply of Internet porn.

# James I, King of England
## (1566–1625)

English poets from the mid-seventeenth-century onward owe a tremendous debt to King James I: He commissioned the King James Bible, an inexhaustible trove of poetic language bound to resonate with churchgoing readers. But in the years before he turned his attention to the word of God, James's abiding fascination was with the devil and his minions; that is, with *witches*.

In 1590, while he was still King James VI of Scot-

land, he immersed himself in a bizarre witch hunt that began with the routine denunciation of a midwife (she'd made the mistake of healing the sick and staying out late at night). Soon enough some seventy witches had been rounded up and a fiendish plot revealed: The coven had stirred up tempests meant to sink the ship in which the king was sailing home from Denmark with his new bride, Queen Anne.

James personally oversaw the questioning of a schoolmaster known as Dr. Fian. In order to elicit the required testimony, the subject's head was jerked violently with a rope. He was fitted with "the bootes," viselike contraptions designed to squeeze the calves. The nails were yanked from his fingers with pincers. The bootes were reapplied, and his legs crushed.

Dr. Fian was eventually executed, his mangled body publicly burned.

Six years later, James published his *Daemonologie,* in which he shared with the world his hard-earned witchcraft wisdom. In a nutshell: "Loath they are to confess without torture, which witnesseth their guiltiness."

# Tom Cruise
## (b. 1962)

For a scary moment in the summer of 2005, it looked as though Tom Cruise might be going off the rails.

The early warning sign came when he insisted on having a tent staffed with "volunteer Scientology ministers" on the set of *War of the Worlds* (they were there, he said, "to help the sick and injured"). By April, he was exchanging sharp words with an interviewer from *Der Spiegel* who made the mistake of uttering the word "pseudoscience." (This was after Cruise had insisted that he himself had "helped hundreds of people get off drugs," and that Scientology has "the only successful drug rehabilitation program in the world.")

Then there was the Brooke Shields fiasco: Scientology considers modern psychiatry and its medications to be a menace; Brooke admitted to popping pills to treat her postpartum depression, and so tactful Tom publicly chastised her (and added that her career had tanked).

Then came the "couch incident"—the forty-two-year-old Cruise leaping all over Oprah's furniture, professing undying love for his twenty-six-year-old squeeze, Katie Holmes.

Suddenly everyone was asking, will Scientology sink the most powerful actor in Hollywood?

Apparently not. Even though it's been revealed that Cruise is the Scientology No. 2, and anyone with access to the Web and the slightest curiosity has seen his kooky-scary ravings about his creepy cult ("we are the way to happiness, we bring peace and unite cultures")—he's still a big-time box office draw.

# William Butler Yeats
## (1865–1939)

When the young William Butler Yeats attended his first séance, it was a jolting experience: His body, he recalled, "moved like a suddenly unrolled watch-spring"—he was thrown back against the wall; he rapped the table with the knuckles of his neighbor's hand. He tried to pray, to ward off evil

spirits—but out of his mouth instead came lines from *Paradise Lost.*

Fast forward three decades to Yeats's honeymoon. He's fifty-two; his bride, George Hyde-Lees, is twenty-five. Yeats (who'd been in love with one woman, Maude Gonne, for most of his adult life, and had also proposed, two months earlier, to Maude's daughter, Iseult) was in crisis, wracked with worry that his marriage was a mistake. But then, on day four of the honeymoon, clever George developed a new and useful talent: automatic writing. She became a conduit to the spirit world: Yeats would ask questions, and the pen in George's hands would provide the answers. Yeats had found happiness at last.

George's automatic writing sessions (four hundred of them in all, producing some four thousand pages) gave Yeats the framework for his "system"—the vast architecture of "gyres" and "phases" that he codified in that famously impenetrable mystic credo *The Vision.*

To his publisher, Yeats said, "I dare say I delude myself in thinking this book is my book of books." (It bombed.)

He was the best poet of the twentieth century—and the most easily misled.  ⸙

# Mother Ann Lee
## (1736–84)

In a prison cell in Manchester, England, Ann Lee had a vision: She saw a copulating Adam and Eve tossed out of the Garden of Eden by a disgusted deity. From this she concluded that the original sin was not disobedience but sex. And if hanky-panky displeased the Supreme Being, then celibacy must delight Him. Hence the Shakers, the religious sect that flourished until its own founding principle brought about an inevitable decline.

The charismatic leader of a tiny sect of "Shaking Quakers," Lee had other visions: Jesus appeared to her and let her know that she was Himself made flesh—a living, female counterpart to Christ. It was also revealed to her that she should leave England for America; she and eight followers landed in New York City in 1774.

Celibacy continued to be the ideological core of the sect. Fierce in her condemnation of lust in all its guises (except ecstatic dancing, of course, and the obscure gratification of speaking in tongues), Lee's antisexual ardor is said to have begun in childhood. Her extreme feelings about fornication could only have been confirmed by a marriage she'd done her level best to avoid, four stillbirths, and the death of four other children in infancy.

The downside of celibacy (practiced successfully, it leads to extinction), Mother Lee ignored. From a peak of six thousand in the early nineteenth century, the Shaker population has dwindled drastically—only four remain.

# Bush and Co.

Take a man with a troubled past eager to convince himself of his special role in history, a man who gambles on gut instinct and then chooses to see the gamble as destiny in the making; now drop that man into the Oval Office, proclaim him commander in chief, and surround him with clever, manipulative advisers, each one equipped with a private cache of certitude. It's a perfect storm. It's the presidency of George W. Bush.

On April 18, 2006, George W. Bush proclaimed, "I'm the decider, and I decide what is best." He'd been in the White House for six years, and at last he'd uttered

the phrase that revealed precisely the deep logic of his behavior. Beginning with status conferred by others—by the Bush and Walker families, say, or by the Supreme Court—"I'm the decider" is the naked, narcissistic "I" dressed up with authority, the spoiled, stubborn son of privilege in the role of resolute leader. "I decide what is best" is the reality he makes: Because he's the decider, he decides, and because he has decided, what he has decided is best. Doubt doesn't enter into the equation—it's excluded by the perfect circularity of the logic. Second thoughts are for wimps. Welcome to Iraq.

Among his enablers, Dick Cheney takes pride of place. Working W.'s oedipal weakness with ruthless cunning, Cheney offered his puppet an irresistible prize: expanded presidential powers. (How could the son fail to grasp the underlying message: "You will be greater than your father"?) Cheney also opened the door to his old neocon pals, Paul Wolfowitz and Richard Perle, who seized the opportunity presented by 9/11 to implant in Bush their unshakable dogma about projecting America's power around the globe and establishing democracy in the Middle East. And Cheney, remember, was an expert on WMD.

But let's not forget Karl Rove, "Boy Genius," whose dream of enduring Republican dominance meant persuading Bush that the Rove brand of partisan politics was the key to a successful, *two*-term presidency. (Take that, Dad!) Rove's presence in the West Wing meant that

George W.'s domestic policy lurched to the right at every crucial juncture; and in the wake of 9/11, he made sure that the threat of terrorist strikes would become a handy weapon in the Republican arsenal.

Last, least, but not wholly without blame, Condoleezza Rice, who developed a kind of freaky empathy, sensing the burgeoning certainties of her boss and echoing them precisely, so that she seemed almost to anticipate his next unswerving conviction.

Neither George Bush nor his cronies ever admitted to error. Even after his popularity plummeted and his presidency was declared moribund, the president himself continued to radiate untroubled confidence in his own immaculate judgment.

# André Maginot
## (1877–1932)

When your last name is attached to one of the great failures in the history of military strategy, when, in fact, your name becomes synonymous with misplaced confidence, it's a good idea to sink quietly into obscurity—which is exactly what André Maginot has done in the seven decades since he died (after eating contaminated oysters) at age fifty-five.

A career politician who in 1914 resigned his post as undersecretary of state for war to enlist in the infantry, Maginot was wounded near Verdun and decorated with France's highest military honor. After his childhood home in Lorraine was obliterated by bombardment, he vowed that Alsace-Lorraine would never again suffer invasion. Returning to government service, he dedicated himself to the idea of fortifying the border with Germany.

Maginot turned himself into a relentless lobbyist, agitating year after year for a fixed defensive line, modern and impenetrable. (Charles de Gaulle was among the prominent opponents of the scheme, preferring to spend more on tanks and combat aircraft.) Eventually, in 1929, Maginot browbeat the Assemblée Nationale into allocating 3.3 billion francs for his complex of concrete forts, proving again the power of single-minded persistence.

Perhaps it's just as well that he didn't live to see the consequence of his valiant determination. In 1940, the German Blitzkrieg simply circumvented the Maginot Line, driving through Belgium toward Dunkirk and through the Ardennes down to Paris. The ingenious fortifications proved useless: France fell in just six weeks.

# Sam Goldwyn
## (1879–1974)

Talent, like beauty, is in the eye of the beholder. Unless of course the beholder is the all-powerful boss of a movie studio that bears his name, in which case beauty and talent are plentiful wherever he says. Especially if he's the kind of guy who likes to boast, "I am willing to admit that I may not always be right, but I am never wrong."

When Sam Goldwyn decided that he had found the next Garbo in a Russian actress named Anna Sten (née Anel Sudakevich), nothing could persuade him otherwise. He brought her to Hollywood and began an expensive and bootless eighteen-month makeover. First she had to learn English, then Hollywood-style acting (before Goldwyn discovered her, she'd already been discovered, at age fifteen, by Stanislavski, who left his mark). Goldwyn launched a million-dollar publicity campaign to prepare audiences for her first American movie, a loose

adaptation of Emile Zola's *Nana*. The film premiered in New York in February of 1934. It flopped. Goldwyn refused to give up. In the same year he produced *We Live Again*—another flop. Finally he paired Anna with Gary Cooper, but that didn't work, either. American audiences refused to fall in love, and Sten became known as "Goldwyn's folly."

The irony is that she was actually a good actress—she just wasn't Greta Garbo, even if Sam Goldwyn said so.

# Thomas Wentworth Higginson
## (1823–1911)

Thomas Wentworth Higginson was no dope: A talented essayist, he engaged in lively polemics in the leading magazines of his day. Nor was he small-minded: An ardent feminist, he was already a prominent champion of women's suffrage more than half a century before the passage of the 19th Amendment. No one ever accused him of being a hidebound conservative: A militant abolitionist, he led the first black regiment in the Civil War.

And yet he could not bring himself to believe that the world was ready for Emily Dickinson's wildly odd and original poetry.

Dickinson wrote to him in 1862, enclosing four poems and asking, "Are you too deeply occupied to say if my Verse is alive?" He was not too busy, and his answer must have encouraged her (we only have her half of the correspondence), for this was the start of a twenty-five-year epistolary dalliance, flirtatious but chaste (they met only twice). From the beginning he urged that she "delay" publication.

Thanks to Dickinson's own ambivalence, the delay lasted until four years after her death, when her family asked Higginson to help edit a volume of her poetry. He agreed. But the edition he published in 1890 ironed out the meter, regularized the punctuation—removing those distinctive dashes—and simply dropped passages deemed ungainly or obscure. In other words, he published shrink-wrapped Dickinson packaged for a late-Victorian audience.

Sixty-five years passed before an undoctored edition of her poetry became available.

# Nelson Bunker Hunt
## (b. 1926)
# and
# William Herbert Hunt
## (b. 1929)

Pity poor Bunker and Herbert Hunt, two sons of Texas oil magnate H. L. Hunt. In the late 1960s, the brothers Hunt were among the richest men in the world; by the late '80s, after the family oil business went under—having been fatally weakened first by a crackpot silver scam and then by the crash in oil prices—Bunker and Herbert had together lost an estimated $5 billion. But as Bunker famously said, "A billion dollars isn't what it used to be."

Trying to corner the market in silver when you're already insanely rich is strange—but what's stranger still is the psychological motivation at work. Bunker was the idea man, Herbert took care of the details, and Bunker thought of silver as a tangible, inflation-proof safeguard against the encroaching communist threat: When Western economies collapsed under pressure from the atheistic agents of communism, the brothers Hunt would be sitting pretty on top of their hoard of silver (9 percent of the world supply—which they stashed, by the way, in Switzerland, flying it over on 707s with Texas cowboys riding shotgun).

But they didn't just hoard the silver, which is what any normal right-wing crazy would do. They tried to manipulate the price, buying contracts *on margin* and driving the market up and up and up—until at last it crashed on "Silver Thursday" (March 27, 1980) and did more damage to the Hunts' fortune than any commie could ever have dreamed.

# John Wayne
## (1907–79)

As American as John Wayne.... Well, of course "American" meant something narrower, something whiter in the 1940s when Marion "Duke" Morrison became a bona fide Hollywood star and began to stake his claim to a rugged, manly corner of the national psyche. His public image was all apple pie patriotism—conservative, Republican, staunchly anticommunist—but in his private life, he had an urge, a compulsion, even, to embrace the exotic Other.

He married three times. His first wife, Josephine

Saenz, was the daughter of the Panamanian consul general in Los Angeles; of their divorce (after four children) Wayne said, "It was the stupidest damn thing I ever did in my life." Except, perhaps, marrying wife No. 2, Esperanza Baur Díaz Ceballos (nicknamed "Chata"), whom he met in Mexico City. He imported the voluptuous Chata (along with her mother) to Los Angeles, where the rumors that circulated about her past were nearly as ugly as the couple's frequent drunken brawls.

Wayne's third wife, Pilar Palette, was Peruvian.

As he later remarked, "Some men collect stamps; I go for Latin Americans."

He did have affairs with women who were emphatically *not* Latin American—Marlene Dietrich, say—but his fixed idea of marital bliss was to get hitched with a Hispanic woman, a conviction that seems all the more peculiar when you consider that every time he ended up divorced, and that his second marriage was a screaming, tabloid-fodder disaster ("like shaking two volatile chemicals in a jar," Wayne later said).

# Girolamo Savonarola
## (1452–98)

"It would be good for religion if many books that seem useful were destroyed," declared Savonarola, the Dominican friar who ruled Florence in the last decade of the fifteenth century. "When there were not so many books and not so many arguments and disputes, religion grew more quickly than it has since." We all know Savonarola's preferred method for disposing of offending texts: his infamous Bonfire of the Vanities, a huge pyre of paintings (especially nudes), sculptures (ditto), musical instruments, mirrors, women's finery—and of course books. He envisioned a Florentine theocracy dedicated to perfecting the righteousness of the people—whether they liked it or not. Culture would be policed by the monks, education dispensed by them. As for public morality, Savonarola outlawed homosexuality and made sodomy a capital offense. He wanted, in sum, to strip all ornament from the Renaissance, and

refocus attention on salvation. Thanks to incandescent sermons and the odd prophecy that seemed to come true, he inspired fervent devotion in his followers—but the fickle crowds eventually tired of his rigor, his power ebbed, and he was arrested for heresy.

Two ironies: Savonarola, notorious burner of books, was also a prolific publisher of pamphlets, which he used to spread political propaganda. And he himself was burned at the stake in the Piazza della Signoria—the same square where he had incinerated the "immoral" works of great poets and artists.

# Walt Whitman Rostow
## (1916–2003)

Among the best and brightest who brought us the Vietnam War, Walt Rostow stands out as the presidential adviser who never hesitated, never reconsidered, and certainly never expressed regret. An economist who became a speechwriter for John Kennedy, Rostow served as a national security adviser to Lyndon Johnson.

When Averell Harriman dubbed him "America's Rasputin," Harriman had in mind the pernicious influence Rostow exerted over Johnson, but the story begins in 1961, when Rostow advised Kennedy that he should be "gearing up the whole Vietnam operation." In 1964 and 1965, he argued for the deployment of U.S. troops in Laos and South Vietnam and for a naval blockade of North Vietnam. By 1966, he was advocating "systemic and sustained bombing" of petroleum installations in Hanoi and Haiphong.

Fiercely anticommunist, adamant about the moral justification for the war, and impervious to criticism, he pushed for escalation at every juncture. He was so confident of an American victory that not even defeat—and the death of more than fifty-eight thousand U.S. soldiers—changed his mind.

In 1986, asked about his role in shaping the Johnson administration's Vietnam strategy, Rostow replied, "I don't spend much time worrying about that period."

A decade later, when former defense secretary Robert McNamara apologized (almost) for his role in the "tragedy" of the war, Rostow responded by saying: "We certainly lost the battle, the test of will, in Vietnam, but we won the war in Southeast Asia."

# Henry Ford
## (1863–1947)

Until about 1918—by which time roughly half the cars in the United States were Model Ts—Henry Ford focused with monomaniacal intensity on the production of his automobile. After that, his attention wandered. He bought a newspaper, the *Dearborn Independent,* and, beginning in May 1920, used it to indulge a new hobby: spreading anti-Semitic propaganda. Under the rubric "The International Jew: The World's Foremost Problem," his paper spewed a noxious mix of slander and paranoid nonsense. Ford, it seems, had fallen under the influence of that infamous, unstoppable hoax *The Protocols of the Elders of Zion,* which purports to be the master plan for Jewish world domination, to be achieved through economic chicanery and the dissemination of pornographic literature. In 1920, Ford sponsored the printing of five hundred thousand copies. Though the *Protocols* were comprehensively

debunked in 1921, he remained a true believer and continued to cite them as proof of Jewish perfidy: "The only statement I care to make about the *Protocols*," he said that same year, "is that they fit in with what is going on. They are sixteen years old, and they have fitted the world situation up to this time." Is it any wonder that he made friends among the world's most virulent anti-Semites? "I regard Henry Ford as my inspiration," Adolf Hitler told a *Detroit News* reporter in 1931, adding that he kept a life-size portrait of the American automaker next to his desk. ·

# Mary Baker Eddy
## (1821–1910)

There's something spooky about the fact that even her most virulent critics refer to Mary Baker Eddy as "Mrs. Eddy"—as though she might smite them from beyond the grave if they lapse into disrespectful informality. Never mind that Eddy was the name of her third husband, Asa Gilbert Eddy, a sewing machine salesman to whom she was married for six years until his death in 1892—in the vast literature, pro and con, the founder of Christian Science is Mrs. Eddy.

According to the postmortem, her husband died

of heart failure, but Mrs. Eddy—whose faith denies the reality of sickness, death, and sin—had other ideas. "I know it was poison that killed him," she declared, "not material poison but mesmeric poison."

This is the scary flip side of faith healing: If good vibes can heal, bad vibes can harm. In her later years, when Mrs. Eddy grew increasingly preoccupied by what she called "malicious animal magnetism" (a kind of black magic directed at her by enemies and critics), she surrounded herself with loyal acolytes whose job it was to ward off evil emanations through prayer.

It's surprising that she needed any help at all. An early biographer reports that Mrs. Eddy had a commanding technique for settling disagreements: Drawing up her shoulders, she would look her adversary in the eye and say very slowly, "God has directed me in this matter. Have you anything further to say?"

# James Jesus Angleton
## (1917–87)

There was only ever one certainty in James Angleton's world: No one can be trusted. The chief of counterintelligence at the CIA for twenty years, Angleton is now associated in the popular imagination with this Kafkaesque motto: "Deception is a state of mind and the mind of the state." He's remembered by his colleagues as a paranoid workaholic, tirelessly vigilant, chain-smoking Virginia Slims, obsessed with the idea that the KGB had "compromised" the CIA. In brief, he was haunted by the fear of moles.

How did the poor guy get that way?

He had been the protégé of Kim Philby, the notorious British spymaster who defected to the Soviet Union in 1963. Philby was one of the British agents who instructed the young Angleton in the dark arts of espionage—and all the while the tutor was a mole. Later, Angleton became the unwitting source of top-secret in-

formation Philby passed to the Russians. The betrayal left permanent scars.

There's a long, comical list of statesmen Angleton suspected of spying for the Communists, among them the prime ministers of Canada, Sweden, and the United Kingdom, the chancellor of West Germany—and even Henry Kissinger.

But the more serious consequence of Angleton's paranoia was the sinister climate of fear and suspicion within the CIA itself, which resulted in a crowning irony: James Angleton himself was suspected of being a double agent.

# Henning von Holtzendorff
## (1853–1919)

By the end of 1916, Germany and the Allies had fought to a bloody standstill. There was a real danger, Admiral Henning von Holtzendorff told Kaiser Wilhelm II, that the war would end "in the mutual exhaustion of all parties"—which, the admiral hastened to add, would be "a disaster for us." Only victory would assure Germany's future as a world power.

But von Holtzendorff had a plan: Break England's backbone with "the submarine weapon." He was convinced that his U-boats could sink six hundred thousand tons a month of the shipping bound for British ports. As a result of the blockade, he promised, England would be "gasping in the reeds like a fish"; the Allies would sue for peace within six months.

There was a catch: A declaration of unrestricted submarine warfare would surely bring the United States into the war. Not a problem, countered von Holtzendorff: England will capitulate before the Americans manage to muster their forces and transport them across the Atlantic. He told the kaiser, "I will give Your Majesty my word as an officer that not one American will land on the Continent." The kaiser believed him.

Germany unleashed its U-boats on February 1, 1917, exacting a terrible toll and causing the United States to declare war on April 6. The British did not capitulate, and the Americans landed more than 2 million troops in Europe. Eight months after the first American offensive, Germany surrendered.

# Elijah Muhammad
## (1897–1975)

Supreme Minister of the Nation of Islam for more than forty years, Elijah Muhammad (né Elijah Poole in Sandersville, Georgia) was largely responsible for elaborating and disseminating a refreshingly unusual racial doctrine. He taught that black people are descended from an aboriginal tribe called Shabazz that's been around for at least 66 trillion years, since before the earth and moon were sundered by a tremendous blast. White people are of more recent vintage: They were created about seven thousand years ago by a mad scientist called Yakub who grafted the "black germ" to a "white germ" and thereby gave birth to the Caucasoid race. Apparently some six hundred years passed before Yakub and his coconspirators achieved the pinky gray color we call white—but whatever the exact hue, the Caucasians were bad news: Elijah Muhammad lumped the "blue-eyed devils" together with "the ser-

pent, the dragon...and Satan—all mean one and the same." The white devils usurped the proper place of the black people, but Elijah Muhammad prophesied a return to black supremacy. (According to his doctrine, all of history has already been written by twenty-four black scientists, supervised by a twenty-fifth.)

Did Elijah Muhammad mellow in his old age? Apparently not. Asked a few years before his death whether each and every white was truly a blue-eyed devil, he replied, "Whether they are actually blue-eyed or not, if they are actually one of the members of that race they are devils."

# Delia Salter Bacon
## (1811–59)

As Nathaniel Hawthorne remarked after telling the tale of Delia Bacon: "This has been too sad a story." Brilliant, penniless, and therefore obliged to live by her wits, Delia Bacon was eventually betrayed by her own cleverness. Convinced that the plays of Shakespeare were written by a conclave of Elizabethan luminaries presided over by Francis Bacon (no relation), she believed, moreover, that the plays were written in code to conceal a subversive political philosophy.

Ralph Waldo Emerson encouraged Bacon to pursue her research in Shakespeare's native land; she wrote to him gratefully, "Be assured, dear sir, there is no possibility of a doubt as to the main points of my theory." She sailed for England in 1853, furnished with letters of introduction to Emerson's friend Thomas Carlyle. (Carlyle invited her to tea; afterward he wrote to Emerson, "I have not in my life seen anything so tragically quixotic as her Shakespeare enterprise.")

Hawthorne, who was American consul in Liverpool at the time, recognized that she was a "monomaniac" caught in "a prodigious error," yet nonetheless helped her publish her huge, impenetrable tract. It was ridiculed by the few critics who noticed it, but Bacon was probably unaware of the savage reception it received—she was already slipping into madness, and died two years later in an insane asylum.

To this day doubters insist that Shakespeare—"that wretched player," Bacon called him—could never have written his thirty-eight plays.

# John Brown
## (1800–59)

"Misguided fanatic"—
that's what Abraham Lincoln called him, and certainly, any dispassionate consideration of his blood-soaked career from Pottawatomie onward would lead to the same conclusion: John Brown was a terrorist, convinced of the efficacy of violence. But others saw him as a man prepared to die for a high moral principle, the abolition of slavery. "The bravest and humanest man in all the country"—that's what Henry David Thoreau called him. "I rejoice that I live in this age, that I am his contemporary."

Consider Brown's last public statement, made on the day he was executed by the state of Virginia for the failed raid on Harpers Ferry (which resulted in the death of seventeen men, among them two of his own sons): "I, John Brown, am now quite certain that the crimes of this guilty land will never be purged away but with blood. I

had, as I now think, vainly flattered myself that without very much bloodshed it might be done." Lunacy or prophecy? Both, we think.

You didn't need a crystal ball to see in 1859 that the country was headed for civil war; but to believe, without the least tremor of doubt, that capturing the Harpers Ferry armory with nineteen men and distributing its one hundred thousand muskets and rifles to the local slaves would set off a chain reaction, unchaining the chattel of the South, and thereby ridding the nation of the "peculiar institution" —now *that's* crazy.

# John Charles Hagee
## (b. 1940)

The televangelist Rev. John Hagee, founder and senior pastor of the Cornerstone Church of San Antonio, Texas, has many peculiar beliefs—about gays, say (responsible for Hurricane Katrina), and the Catholic Church (Hitler's willing partner in the extermination of Jews). But his core convictions concern the End Times, and those convictions have made him one of Israel's staunchest allies.

Mr. Hagee is today's most prominent Christian Zionist (he helped found an organization called Christians United for Israel). When he's prodded by the press (a.k.a. biased mainstream liberal media), he insists that his support of Israel "has nothing to do with any kind of 'end times' Bible scenario." His denials strain credulity; even a cursory examination of his extensive bibliography reveals the nature of his twin fixation: *The Beginning of the End* (1996), *Final Dawn over Jerusalem* (1998), *The Battle for Jerusalem* (2001), *Jerusalem Countdown* (2005).

But Mr. Hagee isn't content to map apocalyptic scriptural prophecy onto current events—he cheerfully invokes a supreme being active in current geopolitical crises. In July of 2006, for instance, in the midst of the Israeli invasion of Lebanon, he declared that support for Israel was "God's foreign policy." He sees no need for negotiation between Israelis and Palestinians. "God," he insists, "is going to supernaturally protect the Jewish people." But just in case God's caught napping, Mr. Hagee would like Israel to hurry up and bomb Iran.

# Rudyard Kipling
## (1865–1936)

War had been declared, and Rudyard Kipling's son Jack was eager to fight. But because Jack was nearsighted, his application for an officer's commission was turned down. So the famous father stepped in to assist. He tapped an old friend, a colonel in the Irish Guards, for a favor, and by mid-September 1914, young Jack was reporting for duty to a barracks in Essex. A year later, six weeks after his eighteenth birthday, Lieutenant Kipling was killed in action at the Battle of Loos.

Jack had been more than willing to go to war, but his patriotic valor was nothing compared with his father's rabid enthusiasm. The great booster of the British Empire was also a furious enemy of Germany. Both a consumer and a disseminator of propaganda about the "atrocities" the kaiser's army had inflicted on the population of Belgium, Kipling published pamphlets under

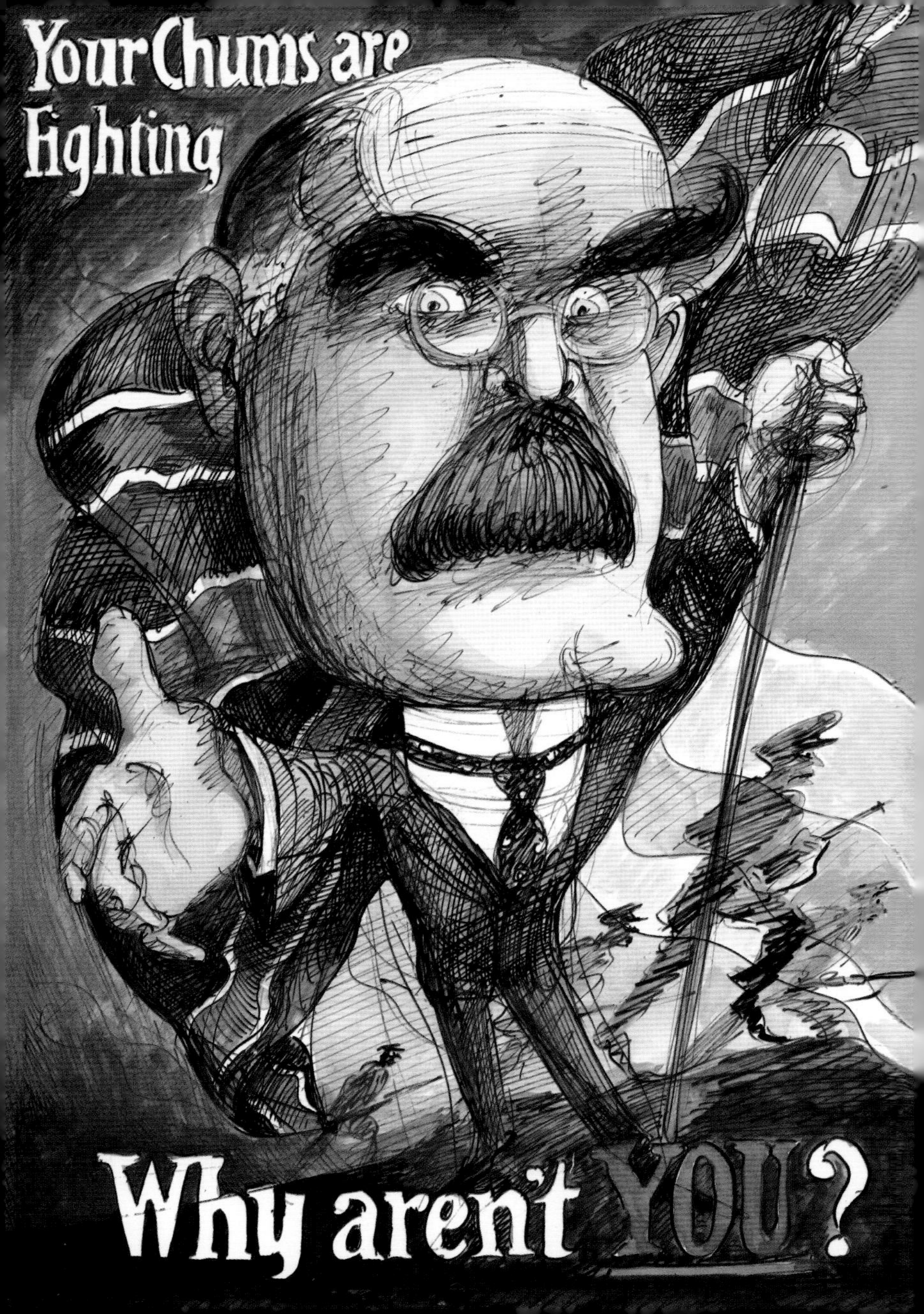
Your Chums are
Fighting
Why aren't YOU?

the auspices of the War Propaganda Bureau and gave speeches at recruiting rallies. At one such event, a month before his son was shipped to France, Kipling declared, "There is no crime, no cruelty, no abomination that the mind of man can conceive which the German has not perpetrated, is not perpetrating, and will not perpetrate if he is allowed to go on."

Here's the question: Could one read Kipling's post-war poem "Common Form"—which is more frequently glossed as a denunciation of politicians who claimed that Britain was adequately armed against the German threat—as a rueful epitaph for his boy Jack?

*If any question why we died,*
*Tell them, because our fathers lied.*

# William Jennings Bryan
## (1860–1925)

When the Tennessee legislature banned the teaching of evolution in every public classroom in the state, William Jennings Bryan fired off a congratulatory telegram to the governor: "The Christian parents of the state owe you a debt of gratitude for saving their children from the poisonous influence of an unproven hypothesis."

Bryan is as famous for his eloquence as for his implacable opposition to Darwinism. The silver-tongued statesman who declared that "all the ills from which America suffers can be traced to the teaching of evolution" should therefore be allowed to speak for himself:

"Evolution seems to close the heart to some of the plainest spiritual truths while it opens the mind to the wildest guesses advanced in the name of science."

"There is no more reason to believe that man descended from some inferior animal than there is to believe that a stately mansion has descended from a small cottage."

"It is better to trust in the Rock of Ages than to know the ages of rock."

"I would rather begin with God and reason down than begin with a piece of dirt and reason up."

"If we have to give up either religion or education, we should give up education."

Remember the Scopes Trial? (One wag had it that Clarence Darrow "made a monkey out of" Bryan.) Five days after the verdict, Bryan died in his sleep. His tombstone reads, "He kept the Faith."

# Aimee Semple McPherson
## (1890–1944)

There's no business like show business—except maybe God's business, and for Aimee Semple McPherson, the two were one and the same. When at last she settled down after years of itinerant preaching, she turned her Angelus Temple into a venue for the most engrossing religious spectacle of her time. McPherson was both the first woman to preach a sermon over the radio and the first woman in the country to be granted a broadcast license (for KFSG in Los Angeles, as in Foursquare Gospel, the name of her church), but really she was happy to use any medium at all to spread the good word. Like her spiritual twin, P. T. Barnum, she was firm in her faith that there's no such thing as bad publicity.

Of which she got plenty. On May 18, 1926, McPherson went for a swim at Ocean Park beach in Santa Monica—and disappeared. It was assumed that

she'd drowned. The faithful mourned. But thirty-five days later, she turned up just over the border in Mexico, telling a fabulous tale of kidnap, torture, and dramatic escape. It seems more likely that she was enjoying a fling with her married lover (a radio engineer for KFSG), but despite a grand jury investigation and plenty of muckraking, no one has ever established the truth.

McPherson never recanted. She never even adjusted the more incredible details. As she repeatedly told reporters throughout the six weeks of white-hot scandal, "That's my story, boys, and I'm sticking with it."

# Winston Churchill
## (1874–1965)

It's hard to argue with Isaiah Berlin, who called Winston Churchill "the largest human being of our time"—but the mythic stature of the hero who saved his nation in World War II shouldn't blind us to his epic blunders. Though he once confided to H. H. Asquith that his life's ambition was "to command great victorious armies in battle," history suggests that he should have left the fighting to the generals.

Remember Gallipoli? Churchill's plans for a naval attack on the Dardanelles in April 1915 resulted in complete catastrophe: twenty-one thousand British troops killed; zero tactical gain. (A historical footnote too odd to ignore: The disastrously faulty intelligence concerning Turkish troop strength was provided by another mythic figure, Lieutenant T. E. Lawrence, a.k.a. "Lawrence of Arabia.") In the aftermath of the Gallipoli debacle, Churchill was removed from his job as First Lord of the Admiralty and given the less critical cabinet role of Chancellor of the Duchy of Lancaster; he soon resigned and took up the command of an infantry battalion on the Western Front.

The next world war found Winston once again First Lord of the Admiralty, and in early 1940, he was the main architect of the Norway campaign, another disaster for the Allies—but this time Winnie escaped censure. Indeed, when a vote of no confidence after the Norway fiasco ousted Neville Chamberlain as prime minister, it was Churchill who took his place. Just in time for his finest hour.

# Lincoln Steffens
## (1866–1936)

"**I**'ve seen the future, and it works"—that one, spectacularly misguided pronouncement has guaranteed immortality to Lincoln Steffens, a muckraking journalist whose other accomplishments (among them a splendid, utterly unreliable autobiography) are fast receding into the haze of neglected history.

Steffens's remark—which he repeated again and again in various versions—was his judgment on Soviet Russia, where he went in 1919, tagging along with an American emissary to the Bolshevik camp. The country was then still in the throes of civil war, but Steffens was confident of the outcome. In Moscow, he interviewed Lenin, and called him a "liberal...the greatest of liberals." He hailed the advent of a new economic and scientific culture that would bring an end to poverty and crime. His euphoric claims about the miraculous efficiency of the Soviet system reached a comical pitch when

he announced in a Paris bar to a group of fellow journalists, "I tell you, they have abolished prostitution"—to which one of his colleagues replied, "My God, Steff! What did you do?"

It comes as no surprise to learn that Steffens's famous phrase was composed before he ever set eyes on the budding promise of the Soviet state in its infancy. He was already at work polishing his mantra aboard the train to Stockholm, days before he made contact with the Bolshevik agents who were to escort him across the frontier and into the future.

# Pope John Paul II
## (1920–2005)

What good is a pope who changes his mind? Karol Józef Wojtyła, who became Pope John Paul II in 1978, published his views on "artificial" contraception in 1960: He was against it. If you find that phrasing flabby, here it is from the horse's mouth: "[C]ontraception is...so profoundly unlawful, as never to be, for any reason, justified." Why? With a prophylactic, the conjugal act—remember, you're *married*—"ceases to be an act of love." Roll on a condom and lovemaking is reduced to mere bodily union.

Only the "natural" kind of contraception is allowed—the periodic continence or intermittent abstinence more familiarly known as the rhythm method.

As a practical matter, John Paul II put the Catholic Church's teaching on contraceptives into a deep freeze during the twenty-six years of his papacy. His insistence on chastity as the only permissible form of birth control would have been merely tragic if AIDS hadn't come along. But twenty-five million people have died of the disease since the early 1980s. In 1993—by which time the pathology of AIDS was common knowledge even in the Holy See—he issued an encyclical restating his absolutist position. As late as 2005—with his dying breath, you might say—he reaffirmed the Vatican's ban on the use of condoms to stop the spread of HIV.

And now he's on the fast track to sainthood.

# Herbert Hoover
## (1874–1964)

In the third volume of his memoirs, *The Great Depression,* Herbert Hoover insists, "I did not say 'Prosperity is just around the corner.'" Maybe not. But look up Hoover on the Web and you'll find that in the popular imagination, the thirty-first president is inextricably linked with confidently asserted optimism.

Could it be that Americans are remembering this 1928 campaign speech? "We in America today are nearer to the final triumph over poverty than ever before in the history of any land. The poor-house is vanishing from among us."

Then the stock market crashed in October of 1929. Weeks later, the president paraded his sangfroid: "Any lack of confidence in the economic future or the basic strength of business in the United States is foolish."

In May of 1930, Hoover declared, "I am convinced

we have passed the worst." A month later, in reply to a delegation requesting a federal public works program, he said, "Gentlemen, you have come sixty days too late. The Depression is over." (Compare that with his memorable phrase "Nobody is actually starving.")

Two hungry years later: "It can be demonstrated that the tide has turned and that the gigantic forces of depression are today in retreat." (That's from a speech delivered on October 22, 1932.) Wrong again.

As any connoisseur of today's faux scandals will tell you, just as damaging as actual misconduct is the *appearance* of misconduct. So, too, with certitude....

# About the Authors

**Adam Begley** has been the books editor of the *New York Observer* since 1996. He's certain of one thing: how lucky he is to share his life in Northamptonshire, England, with his wife, two stepchildren, and three cats.

**Edward Sorel** is the author/illustrator of *Unauthorized Portraits* and *Literary Lives* and is a contributor to *The New Yorker, Vanity Fair,* and the *Nation.* In 2005, he completed his mural for the Waverly Inn in Greenwich Village, reproduced in *The Mural at the Waverly Inn.*